DEC 1 2 2017

W9-AHB-423

NAPA COUNTY LIBRARY
580 COOMBS STREET
NAPA, CA 94559

Goats

Leo Statts

abdopublishing.com

Published by Abdo Zoom™, PO Box 398166, Minneapolis, Minnesota 55439. Copyright © 2017 by Abdo Consulting Group, Inc. International copyrights reserved in all countries. No part of this book may be reproduced in any form without written permission from the publisher. Abdo Zoom™ is a trademark and logo of Abdo Consulting Group, Inc.

Printed in the United States of America, North Mankato, Minnesota
092016
012017

THIS BOOK CONTAINS
RECYCLED MATERIALS

Cover Photo: Borut Trdina/iStockphoto
Interior Photos: Shutterstock Images, 1, 4, 8, 16; Josh Schultz/Shutterstock Images, 5; Yavuz Sariyildiz/ Shutterstock Images, 6; iStockphoto, 7, 14; Daria Borovleva/Shutterstock Images, 9; Radu Bercan/ Shutterstock Images, 10; Dimitry Kalinovsky/Shutterstock Images, 10–11; Dustin Jensen/iStockphoto, 12; Thanakrit Sathavornmanee/Shutterstock Images, 13; Christian Jung/Shutterstock Images, 15; Bartosz Hadyniak/ iStockphoto, 17; Alberto Masnovo/Shutterstock Images, 18; Mandrew Mayovsky/Shutterstock Images, 19; Red Line Editorial, 20 (left), 20 (right), 21 (left), 21 (right)

Editor: Emily Temple
Series Designer: Madeline Berger
Art Direction: Dorothy Toth

Publisher's Cataloging-in-Publication Data
Names: Statts, Leo, author.
Title: Goats / by Leo Statts.
Description: Minneapolis, MN : Abdo Zoom, 2017. | Series: Farm animals |
    Includes bibliographical references and index.
Identifiers: LCCN 2016948666 | ISBN 9781680799057 (lib. bdg.) |
    ISBN 9781624024917 (ebook) | ISBN 9781624025471 (Read-to-me ebook)
Subjects: LCSH: Goats--Juvenile literature.
Classification: DDC 636.3--dc23
LC record available at http://lccn.loc.gov/2016948666

Table of Contents

Goats

Many goats are kept on farms.
People have been keeping goats
for 10,000 years.

But some goats still
live in the wild.

Goats are good climbers.
Their hooves help them
climb without slipping.

In the wild, they can live on steep mountains.

Body

Most goats are black,
brown, or white.

Some have spots or **markings**.

Goats have horns.

They also have beards.

Goats eat leaves and grass.

They also eat grain.
A farmer might feed them hay.
Goats eat salt, too.

Farm Life

Most people raise goats for their milk and meat.

Their milk is also used
to make cheese.

Goats are playful
and friendly animals.

Some people keep
them as pets.

Male goats are called billy goats.

18

Females are called nannies.
A baby goat is called a kid.

Average Height

A goat is shorter than an acoustic guitar.

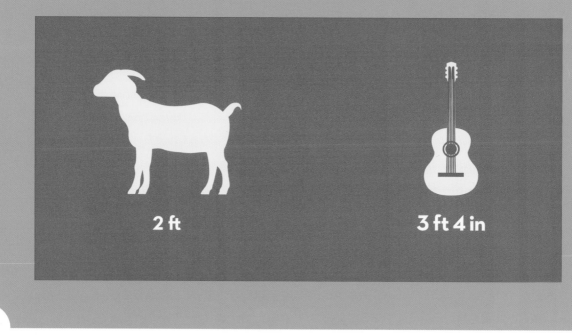

2 ft

3 ft 4 in

Average Weight

A male goat is as heavy as two toilets.

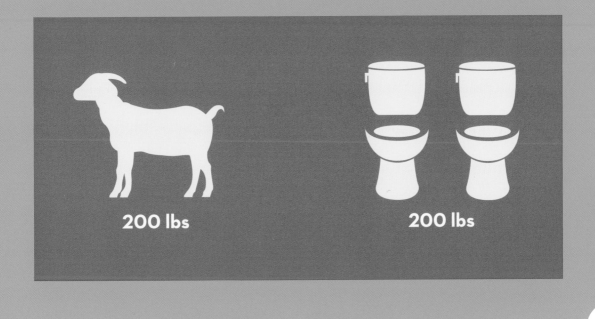

200 lbs   200 lbs

Glossary

grain - the seeds of plants that are used for food.

hooves - hard coverings that protect an animal's feet.

horn - a hard part that grows on the head of some animals.

kid - a baby goat.

marking - a mark or pattern of marks on an animal's fur, feathers, or skin.

Booklinks

For more information
on goats, please visit
booklinks.abdopublishing.com

Zoom In on Animals!

Learn even more with the Abdo Zoom
Animals database. Check out
abdozoom.com for more information.

Index